The Confusing World of Brothers, Sisters and Adoption

The Confusing World of Brothers, Sisters and Adoption

The Adoption Club Therapeutic
Workbook on Siblings

Regina M. Kupecky

Illustrated by Apsley

Jessica Kingsley *Publishers*
London and Philadelphia

First published in 2015
by Jessica Kingsley Publishers
73 Collier Street
London N1 9BE, UK
and
400 Market Street, Suite 400
Philadelphia, PA 19106, USA

www.jkp.com

Library of Congress Cataloging in Publication Data
A CIP catalog record for this book is available from the Library of Congress

British Library Cataloguing in Publication Data
A CIP catalogue record for this book is available from the British Library

ISBN 978-1-84905-764-6
eISBN 978-0-85700-996 8

Printed and bound in Great Britain by Bell & Bain Ltd, Glasgow

INTRODUCTION FOR ADULTS

About this series

This workbook is Book 3 of a series of workbooks about The Adoption Club written for social workers, counselors or therapists working with children aged 5–11, as well as adoptive parents.

The five interactive therapeutic workbooks have been written to address the key emotional and psychological challenges they are likely to experience. They provide an approachable, interactive and playful way to help children to learn about themselves and have fun at the same time.

About this book

The Confusing World of Brothers, Sisters and Adoption is the third book in the Adoption Club series and will explore the different relationships that exist in adoptive families, and the feelings children have about their different siblings.

There are many sibling issues in adoption: separated siblings, half siblings, adopted siblings, unknown siblings and foster siblings, to name a few. Many children do not talk about these siblings because no-one else brings them up. This doesn't mean the children are not thinking about them. This workbook can help children understand the world of siblings and adoption.

Whether you are a parent, a counselor, a therapist, a social worker or a doctor this book will help children by opening their feelings about the adoption world to them. They will no longer feel alone, because they can find a character whose story resemble theirs.

The story brings up many topics, and completing the workbook will probably take many sessions. The coloring and workbook format helps children express their own feelings in a non-threatening way.

Hopefully the workbook will help the child be able to discuss siblings in a healthy way.

If you have questions or need help please drop me an email at ReginaKu@msn.com.

Other workbooks in the Adoption Club series

Book 1: *Let's Learn About Adoption: The Adoption Club Therapeutic Workbook on Adoption and Its Many Different Forms*

Book 2: *How Do We Feel About Adoption? The Adoption Club Therapeutic Workbook on Feelings and Behavior*

Book 4: *Friends, Bullies and Staying Safe: The Adoption Club Therapeutic Workbook on Friendship*

Book 5: *Who We Are and Why We Are Special: The Adoption Club Therapeutic Workbook on Identity*

Meet The Adoption Club!

The Adoption Club is made up of many characters whose lives have been touched by adoption.

Mrs. Bright is the counselor who runs the group.

Mr. Jackman is a history teacher who helps. He was adopted as an infant in a closed adoption. That meant growing up he knew nothing about his birth parents. As an adult he searched for them and found them.

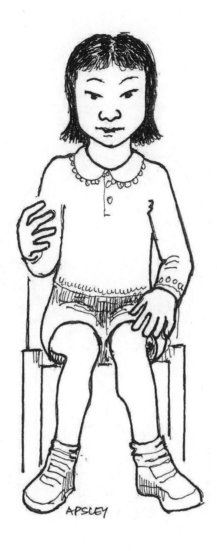

Mary was adopted from China by her single mom. Everyone knows she is adopted because her mom is White and she is Asian. She was three years old when she came to her mom. She is ten right now. She was left by her birth family near the post office in China and then went to an orphanage.

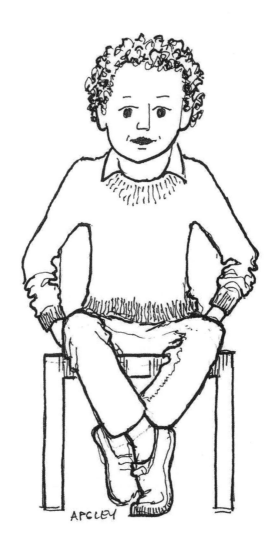

Alexander was adopted from Russia by a single dad. He was
five when he joined his family. He lived in an orphanage too.

Alice was adopted in an open adoption as an infant. Her
birth mother is of Mexican heritage and her birth father is of
Puerto Rican heritage. Her birth parents chose her adoptive
parents. She still visits her birth parents. She is nine and has
one brother who was born to her adoptive parents.

Angela is nine and her birth brother Michael is thirteen. They lived with their birth parents for many years until they went into foster care. Both lived in several homes, and not always together. They have been in their adoptive family for one year. The family adopted two other children before them, who are now four and six.

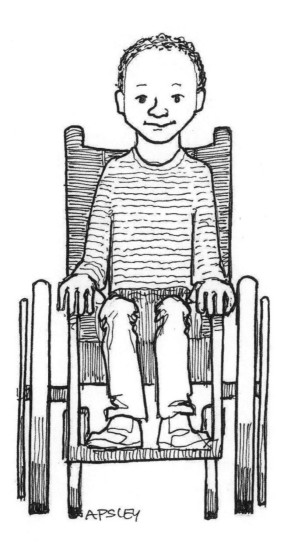

Robert has a disability and needs a wheelchair to get around. He is twelve and was adopted into a kinship adoption, which means he is related to his adoptive family. His adoptive mom is his birth father's sister. They have four birth children and may adopt again. It is a big family.

The Confusing World of Brothers, Sisters and Adoption

Mr. Jackman and Mrs. Bright finished a cup of coffee and began to get ready for The Adoption Club to meet. Tonight, they were going to talk about siblings (brothers and sisters), and they knew the children would have many kinds of siblings as well as many feelings about them.

They hoped the children would learn about the topic as well as be able to talk about their feelings. They both enjoyed their time with The Adoption Club and its members.

"Here they come," said Mr. Jackman, "Alice and her parents are first."

"The rest will be here soon," said Mrs. Bright as she went to the door.

siblings

Alice was followed by Mary, and then Robert and Alexander arrived. Soon Angela and Michael came into the room and everyone got settled.

Mrs. Bright welcomed everyone and began to speak. "Today we are going to talk about brothers and sisters. We can use the word 'sibling' to mean brothers and sisters. There are many kinds of siblings. One type is birth siblings. That means you have the same birth mother and father."

"Like me and Angela," said Michael.

Mr. Jackman asked, "Did you always live together?"

"No," said Michael. "We always lived together with our birth parents. When we were in foster care we mostly lived together. Once we were separated and Angela's foster mother wanted to adopt her and not me. Our social worker said, no, we would be together."

Mrs. Bright said, "Many children, as a matter of fact most children, lose some siblings when they are adopted. You were lucky."

Are you separated from any siblings?

_____

_____

_____

_____

_____

_____

Do you know if you have any?

_____

_____

_____

_____

_____

_____

How do you feel about being separated?

_____

_____

_____

_____

_____

_____

Do you see them?

_____

_____

_____

_____

_____

_____

"The next kind of sibling we are going to talk about is a half sibling," said Mrs. Bright.

Alice giggled. "That sounds funny. Which half? The waist up or waist down? The left side or right side?"

Everyone began to laugh.

"No," Mrs. Bright smiled. "It means you share one parent. When I was a girl I had a half sister. We had the same mother but two different fathers. My mother was divorced after she had me and remarried and had my sister.

"We never said 'half sister' and we still do not. She is the aunt to my children and they call her 'Aunt' not 'half aunt.' We think of ourselves as sisters, siblings, not halves. It has nothing to do with our relationship or how much we care for each other."

Do you have half siblings? Do you know anyone who does?

_____

_____

_____

_____

_____

"You know," said Mary, "I don't know if I have any siblings, half or whole." She looked sad.

Mr. Jackman said, "When I was adopted years ago I didn't know either. I did a search when I was an adult and found I had three half siblings from my birth mother and two from my birth father."

"Unknown siblings can be another kind of sibling," Mrs. Bright said, and she added 'unknown sibling' to the list.

"I think about that sometimes," said Mary. "I wonder if I have any siblings, if they know about me, if I will ever meet them. When I think about it I sometimes get sad. Then I go away by myself."

"Do you ever talk to your adoptive mom about it?" asked Robert.

"No," whispered Mary, "but maybe I should."

Do you ever wonder if you have siblings you do not know about?

_____

_____

_____

_____

How do you feel when you do?

_____

_____

_____

_____

Do you talk to your parents about it?

_____

_____

_____

The room got quiet. All the children were thinking about the unknown. They all had so many unknowns in their lives.

Mrs. Bright continued. "Another kind of sibling is an adopted sibling. You are not biologically related but you are adopted into the same family."

Robert said, "I am the only one adopted into my family right now, but my parents are going to adopt again so I will have an adopted sibling."

Do you have adopted siblings? How many?

_____

_____

_____

_____

_____

_____

In what order did they come into the family?

_____

_____

_____

_____

_____

_____

Robert went on. "Right now, I have four siblings. They were all born into the family so they are full birth siblings. I am the adopted sibling. My aunt and uncle adopted me so I am their adopted brother as well as their birth cousin. When they adopt again that child will be my adopted sibling but not related."

The children smiled. Families can get complicated.

Alice said, "I have a brother—we do not look alike because my parents are Puerto Rican and Mexican. He was born to my parents. I used to think they liked him better because of that. He had more privileges. I finally talked to my parents about it. They explained he had more privileges because he was older. He used to think they loved me more because they chose to adopt me and he just got born. But they love us both the same."

Do you have siblings born to your parents?

Did you ever feel things were not equal?

"Another kind of sibling," said Mr. Jackman, "is a step sibling."

Alice raised her hand. "I have one of those too. I have a brother born to my adopted parents. We live together. My dad was married before and his previous wife had a child. When they got divorced my dad decided to still visit the daughter and his first wife agreed. So she is my step sister. We do not share a parent, she is not adopted, but she is part of my family."

Do you have any step sisters or step brothers?

siblings
half sibling
unknown sibling
adopted sibling
step sibling
foster care
sibling

APSLEY

"One last kind of sibling," said Mrs. Bright, adding it to the chart, "is foster or orphanage siblings. When children are being raised together even though they are not related or adopted into the same family, sometimes children act like the other children are their siblings."

Alexander raised his hand. "That happened to me. I was five when I was adopted. In the orphanage there was a boy named Andrew who was my best friend. I missed him so much when I left. My dad found out he was adopted too and his parents live far from us, but we are allowed to email and talk on the phone. I was so worried about him. I was happy to hear he was safe."

Michael added, "In one foster home I got very close to one of the boys. He was my foster brother and we still talk once in a while."

Do you have any siblings like Michael and Alexander mentioned?

_____

_____

_____

_____

_____

Do you ever worry about some of the children you knew but never see anymore?

_____

_____

_____

_____

_____

The children looked at the chart. They had lots of questions about their birth families, siblings and adopted siblings.

They all needed a break.

When they came back, Mrs. Bright said, "Siblings are important. They are usually the longest relationships we have. When we are adults they provide support, nieces, nephews and cousins for our children. Some siblings are close and some are not. What do your siblings, whatever the kind, teach you?"

Alice raised her hand. "Well, my brother was born to my parents. He is older than me so he teaches me games, helps me with math and tries to order me around!"

Angela said, "Michael has always tried to protect me. When I was scared in foster care he was always by my side." She smiled, and Michael looked embarrassed.

Alexander said, "I am an only child, as far as I know. I think I will tell my dad to adopt again."

Everyone laughed. Alice said, "Be careful what you wish for. Siblings can also be annoying and bossy."

What have you learned from siblings?

_____

_____

_____

_____

_____

_____

What problems have you had from your siblings?

_____

_____

_____

_____

_____

_____

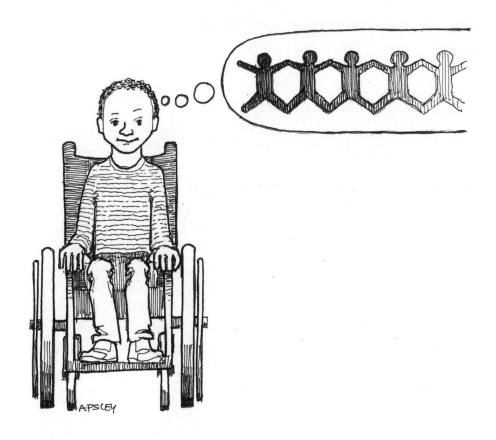

Robert said, "My parents are going to adopt again. I don't know what age, or whether it will be a sister or a brother. Maybe even a small sibling group. I hope they are younger than me, I am tired of being the youngest."

Are you the oldest? Youngest? Middle?

_____

_____

Would you rather be somewhere different in the order?

_____

_____

What do you like/dislike about where you are in the family?

_____

_____

_____

_____

_____

_____

_____

Did the order change when you were adopted?

_____

_____

*Were you the oldest in your birth family but the youngest in
your adoptive family?*

_____

_____

How did that feel?

_____

_____

_____

_____

_____

_____

_____

Mrs. Bright handed out big pieces of paper. "Let's draw our current family," she said.

The children got busy.

"Now on this piece of paper draw the siblings we don't know, we don't know if we have, we never see—siblings we just think about, or who we imagine exist."

Mary immediately drew a boy who was Chinese like her. "I think I have a brother in China," she said. "I don't know; I just think so."

Alexander drew a picture of another boy who looked like him. "I am thinking my birth father and/or mother would have another child by now. He would be my half brother."

Angela drew a picture of a girl younger than herself. "This is a foster sister I had who I really liked."

Robert drew a picture of a girl and a boy. "I imagine that my parents will adopt a brother and sister. They will be full siblings and become my adopted siblings."

Can you draw a picture of who you imagine there might be?

"That was fun," they agreed.

Mr. Jackman said, "Siblings are not always fun. Sometimes they tease us, or take our toys or won't play with us. Sometimes they hit or pinch or shove. You should tell your parents if the hurting gets serious. No one, not even a sibling, has the right to hurt you."

"Yeah," Michael said as he playfully swatted at his sister.

Are your siblings ever harmful by teasing or hurting?

"Siblings can be fun, too. They can play with us, teach us games and help us with homework," Mrs. Bright said. "I even introduced my half sister to her husband."

"Yuck," said Robert who was not into romance.

Everyone laughed.

"When you are adults you will probably attend siblings' weddings, be the aunt or uncle to their children and share both good times and bad. You might live near them or far away, but they are your siblings forever."

"Just like adoption," the children said, "siblings and adoption are forever."

"Even," Mary said thoughtfully, "the ones you never meet. They are still your siblings."

RESOURCES

Your child might enjoy

Bunin, Catherine, Bunin, Sherry and Welch, Sheila Kerry (1992) *Is That Your Sister?* Wayne, PA: Our Children's Press.

Brodzinsky, Anne Braff (2013) *Can I tell you about Adoption?* London, UK: Jessica Kingsley Publishers.

DePaula, Tomie (2002) *A New Barker in The House*. New York, NY: G.P. Putnam's Sons.

Kupecky, Regina and Mitchell, Christine (2009) *A Foster-Adoption Story: Angela and Michael's Journey*. San Francisco, CA. Publisher: Authors.

Adults might enjoy

Keck, Gregory C. and Kupecky, Regina M. (1995; 2009) *Adopting the Hurt Child*. Colorado Springs, CO: Pinon Press.

Kupecky, Regina and Keck, Gregory (1995) *Adopting the Hurt Child*. Colorado Springs, CO: Piñon Press.

Kupecky, Regina and Keck, Gregory (2002) *Parenting the Hurt Child*. Colorado Springs, CO: NavPress.

Kupecky, Regina M. (2004–5) [DVD] *My Brother, My Sister: Sibling Relations in Foster Care and Adoption*. Available by contacting ReginaKu@msn.com or by telephoning (001) 440-230-1960.

James, Arleta (2013) *Welcoming a New Brother or Sister through Adoption*. London, UK: Jessica Kingsley Publishers.

Silverstein, Deborah and Livingston Smith, Susan (2009) *Siblings in Adoption and Foster Care: Traumatic Separations and Honored Connections*. Westport, CT: Praeger Publications.